MW01503316

TEEN PREGNANCY

Why Are Kids Having Babies?

Laurie Rozakis

Twenty-First Century Books

A Division of Henry Holt and Company
New York

Twenty-First Century Books
A division of Henry Holt and Company, Inc.
115 West 18th Street
New York, New York 10011

Henry Holt® and colophon are registered trademarks of Henry Holt and Company, Inc.
Publishers since 1866

©1993 by Blackbirch Graphics, Inc.
First Edition
5 4 3 2 1
Published in Canada by Fitzhenry & Whiteside Ltd.
195 Allstate Parkway, Markham, Ontario, L3R 4T8

Printed in the United States of America

Created and produced in association with Blackbirch Graphics, Inc.

Library of Congress Cataloging-in-Publication Data

Rozakis, Laurie.
    Teen pregnancy: why are kids having babies?/Laurie Rozakis--1st
ed.   p.   cm.--(Issues of our time)
    Includes bibliographical references and index.
    ISBN 0-8050-2569-3 (alk. paper)
    1. Teenage pregnancy--United States--Juvenile literature. 2.
Maternal age--United States--Juvenile literature.   I. Title.
    II. Series.
HQ759.4 .R69   1993
306.7--dc20   93-8516
                                              CIP
                                              AC

Contents

1

......

In Trouble

"There's a basic disrespect for girls who get pregnant. They are still considered lowlifes. People are ashamed of them. They don't want to see them, don't want to know about them, don't want to think kids have sex—but they do," said one 14-year-old mother.

Amy's Story Amy grew up in a well-off family. She lived in an upper-middle-class Chicago neighborhood. Most of her friends were just like her. They lived in nice houses and wore pretty clothes. On weekends they went out and had fun.

Amy had sex for the first time when she was 14 years old. A lot of her friends had started

Pregnant teens face many difficult decisions about the future of their lives. Having a baby usually permanently affects the educational, job, and social opportunities for teenage mothers.

earlier. Every year in health class, Amy's teachers would talk about the female reproductive system. Amy thinks she heard the same lecture about eight times. Despite this, she still didn't understand how a girl got pregnant. She wasn't sure which times were "safe" and which weren't. Her mother wasn't comfortable talking about the subject, and she hadn't seen her father in years. Amy and her girlfriends had some wrong ideas about how to prevent pregnancy—like standing up or dancing right after having sex. Her boyfriend, Chris, told Amy not to worry about it. He was 17 years old and seemed to know what he was doing. He didn't.

When Amy was 15 years old, she got pregnant. Amy didn't tell her mother until she was four months along. She thought that her mother might hit her or throw her out of the house. Her mother did neither. She just started to cry. "My mother gave birth to my older sister when she was just sixteen years old," Amy said. "She always wanted life to be better for me, for things to be easier. She kept crying that my life was all over now."

Amy's grades dropped from B's to D's. "I felt sick all the time. I just couldn't concentrate," she said. "Everyone stared at me. They were talking about me behind my back." Her mother sent her to a maternity home, a place where unwed mothers are cared for until they have their babies. Amy felt better there. Some of the girls at the home were even younger than Amy, and many were planning on keeping their babies. "One of my friends there was only twelve years old," Amy recalls. "She used to watch cartoons on television and laugh." Amy decided that she would keep her baby.

On weekends, Amy would go back home. She planned to get an apartment after the baby was born. If she moved out, she could go on welfare. What about her boyfriend? While Amy was away at the maternity home, he found another girlfriend. About a month before the baby was born, Amy went down to the local welfare office. She applied for Aid to Families with Dependent Children (AFDC). She was very upset and embarrassed to be there. She realized that even with the welfare money, she would barely be able to make ends meet.

At the maternity home, Amy had seen movies about delivering babies. But when it came time to give birth, she wasn't as well prepared as she would have liked. The pain took her by surprise. The nurse gave her an injection to numb the lower half of her body. The pain stopped, but that only gave Amy a chance to think about what was really happening to her. "I kept thinking that there was no going back," she said. "Up to that moment, I never realized what was happening to me." Amy gave birth to a baby girl, whom she named Cindi.

A girlfriend from school came to help Amy with the baby for two weeks. That was fun. "Playing with the baby was like having a doll," Amy said. Then Amy's friend returned to her own life. Amy tried to get back with her old friends, but she soon discovered that they no longer had anything in common with her. "They went out every night," Amy said. "I was tied down with the baby. My life was so different from theirs."

More than half the teenage mothers in America never finish high school, but Amy was determined to get her diploma. She signed up for a special program at the local high school. She had to be up by 5 A.M. to get herself and the baby ready. Then she'd race down to the nursery and run off to her first class. After school, she'd rush home with the baby, play with her for a while, and then hit the books. She also had to prepare dinner, clean the house, do the laundry, and bathe the baby. It was overwhelming.

Amy thought about the future a lot. In the beginning, her girlfriends had come around every day, but now they were back to their own lives. "People like to baby-sit a cute, sleeping infant, but no one wants to chase around a toddler," she said. Amy sometimes gets angry at the baby. "She takes so much time. I don't have a minute to myself. And she costs so much! The diapers, formula, clothing,

Opposite:
Many teen mothers enjoy the "cute" and "cuddly" nature of their babies during the first year. But, as their children grow, mothers are faced with complicated and much more demanding responsibilities.

and toys—I never have a cent!" Amy works hard not to take her anger and frustration out on the baby. Sometimes she wonders if she made a mistake in deciding to keep the child. Maybe she should have put her up for adoption or had an abortion. At times she even wonders if she should or could still call an adoption agency.

Allison's Story

Allison grew up in a religious family. Like most of her friends, she planned to marry sometime after she graduated from high school. She wanted a family right away. She had been going out with Doug for two years. He was rough with her, and once he even slapped her. She found out that she was pregnant in the summer between tenth and eleventh grades. "I think I was glad underneath," she says. "I really didn't know what to do with my life. Maybe the baby would be the answer." She knew that she would have to break up with Doug because of the way he treated her.

Her parents sent her to live with an aunt in a distant town. Her aunt worked all day, and Allison was home by herself. She had a lot of time to think. Allison wanted to keep the baby at first. "My aunt said that we didn't have the money to raise the baby. The more I thought about it, the more I saw that she was right."

The baby was a week late. Allison held her for a moment and then handed her to the nurse. Through her tears, she thought, "This is the right thing for me." She went back home and completed high school. After graduation, she started working as a secretary and met a young man whom she liked a lot. "But he has to understand what I've been through," she said. "It has changed me so much. I'm not the same person I was before."

How many other kids are having kids? How big a problem is it?

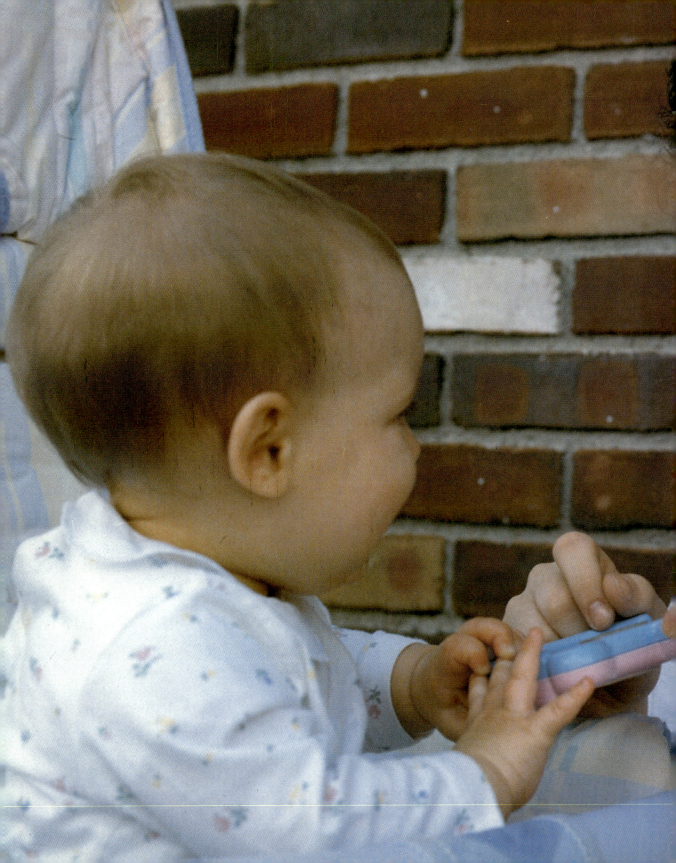

2

Looking at the Numbers

You've just read about two young girls who had babies. Do they represent most teenagers? What do the numbers say? Let's take a look at some of the facts.

Teen Pregnancy Rates in America Today According to the National Survey of Family Growth, in 1984 only 19 percent of girls under the age of 18 were sexually experienced. Today, that number is nearly 50 percent higher. Out of 10 boys, 8 will have had sex by the time they are 18 years old. Three out of 10 girls will be sexually experienced by age 18. Even younger kids are sexually active. Among kids who are 12 and

As America's youth has become sexually active at an increasingly younger age, the number of teen pregnancies—and teen mothers—has also increased significantly.

13 years old, the figure is nearly 1 in 5 boys and 1 in 17 girls. Look around your classroom, and assume that your classmates reflect the national average. If there are 20 students in your class, at least 3 may be having sex by the national standard. That's about 2 of the boys and 1 of the girls.

After 30 years of steady decline, the teen birthrate started to rise again in 1987. Today, 10 percent of American girls become mothers before they have turned 18. Most of the increase is for younger teens, those between the ages of 15 and 17. In 1986, the rate was 30.6 per 1,000 teens. In 1988, it rose to 33.8 per 1,000. There are about 10,000 births a year to girls 15 or younger. In all, 322,000 babies—about one twelfth of the 3.9 million born in 1988—were born to unmarried teenagers. Another 9 percent of teenage girls had abortions. What do these numbers mean? Here is a simple breakdown:

- 3,000 teenage girls become pregnant every day.
- Births to teenagers rose 200 percent between 1960 and 1980.
- More than 1 million teenage girls become pregnant every year.
- Half of the girls who become pregnant each year deliver their babies, which means that 1 in every 30 girls ages 15 to 17 has a baby.
- There is a 44 percent chance that a girl will become pregnant before she turns 20.

Opposite:
Nine-year-old Marta Artunduaga is the youngest mother on record. Here, she lies in a hospital room after giving birth to her baby.

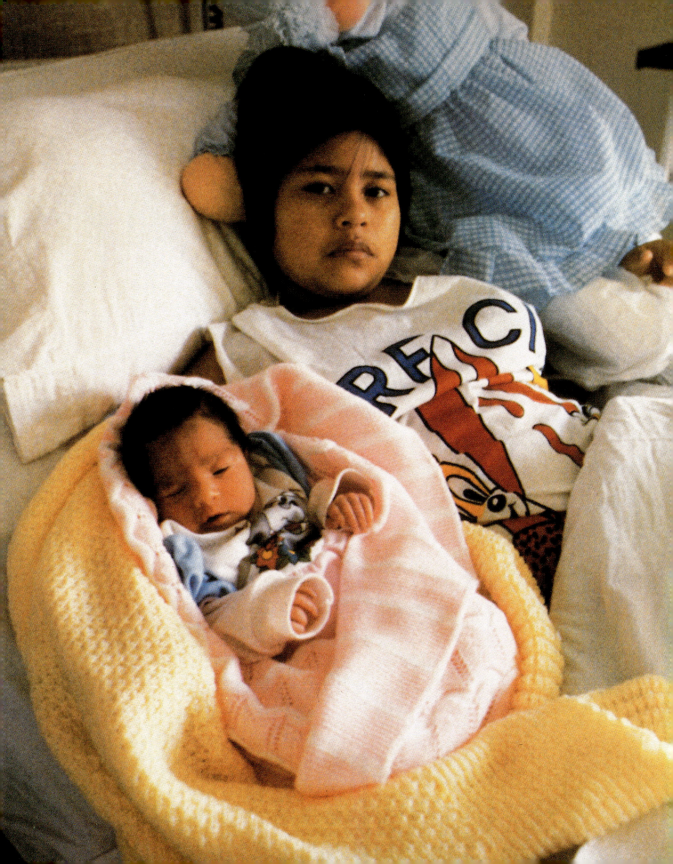

- Forty percent of today's 14-year-old girls will become pregnant by the time they are 19.
- Eight in 10 teenage pregnancies are unplanned.

There are so many pregnant children in America that one study called the situation an epidemic. "Adolescent pregnancy is a problem our nation can no longer afford to ignore," one expert said. How do adults feel about this? A recent poll showed that 95 percent of Americans consider teen pregnancy a very serious problem. This represents an 11 percent increase from 1985. "Something is deeply wrong when our children would rather change diapers than get on with the business of growing up," said one concerned parent. The problem of growing up in our society today is more confusing for kids than ever.

A Changing

Picture Before this increase in childbirths among teens, the peak year for teen childbirths was 1972. That year, more than 230,000 young girls gave birth. Why was this number higher than it would be in succeeding years? Most researchers think it is because this was the year before the U.S. Supreme Court handed down its landmark *Roe* v. *Wade* decision. This case overturned state laws against abortion. After that, more teens all across the country were able to legally end their pregnancies.

Opposite:
For married teens, having a baby means extra work for both parents. In addition to washing clothes and keeping the house clean, they must be able to handle child care and schoolwork, which leaves them little time for anything else.

Births to

Married Teens Tina was 14 when she met Luis. He was 19 and very handsome. He had gone to her home to do some repair work. Tina's mother, who was a widow, thought Luis was a nice young man, and she welcomed him into their home. Tina's mother never realized, however, that Luis was interested in Tina. After all, she was just a child.

When Tina's mother was out, Luis would come to the house, and he and Tina would kiss and make out. Tina couldn't figure out how to keep Luis interested in her. She knew about birth-control devices, but what if her mother found them around the house? Besides, that would make everything seem so planned. She wanted sex with Luis to seem as if she were being "swept away by the moment."

Three months later, Tina became pregnant. She knew right away because she felt sick. Her mother thought it was the flu. Tina went down to the drugstore. She got a home-pregnancy kit. When the results were positive, Tina panicked. "What am I going to do?" she wondered. Finally she decided to tell her mother.

At first her mother was shocked. Then she was very angry. "I'm going to have him arrested and throw you out of the house!" Tina's mother thundered. When she cooled down, she said, "I like Luis. The best way out of this is for the two of you to get married. You can live here and finish school. I will help you raise the baby."

Most teen pregnancies don't end this way today. Thirty years ago, nearly all teen childbirths took place within marriage. Babies of unwed mothers were most often put up for adoption. Of the babies born outside marriage in 1970, for example, half were put up for adoption. All this began to change in the early 1970s. Between 1970 and 1982, the number of babies born outside marriage rose by almost 50 percent. Today, 90 percent of unmarried mothers raise their children. That means that only 10 percent of unwed teenage mothers give their children up for adoption.

Teen Pregnancy Rates in Other Parts of the World
The United Nations estimates that there were 526 million boys and 506 million girls in the world in 1985. About 80 percent of them live in the developing countries of Africa, Asia, and Latin America. They make up about a quarter of the world's population. By the year 2020, the United Nations estimates that there will be 1.3 billion teenagers in the world. That's an increase of 27 percent. Of these, approximately 86 percent will live in developing countries.

How does America stack up against these countries? The United States leads the industrialized

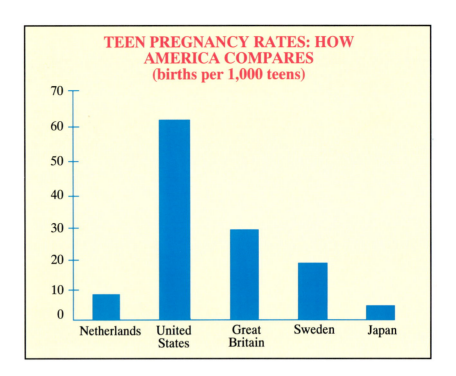

TEEN PREGNANCY RATES: HOW AMERICA COMPARES
(births per 1,000 teens)

world in teen pregnancy and teen-childbirth rates. The teen-pregnancy rate in America is more than double the rate in Great Britain. It's more than triple the rate in Sweden. It's seven times the rate in the Netherlands, where there are 9 teenage births per 1,000. There are only 4 teenage births per 1,000 in Japan. U.S. rates are also higher than those of Italy, China, South Korea, and Portugal. America's teen-childbirth rate is even higher than that of some developing countries, such as Tunisia.

Other developing countries do have higher teen childbirth rates than the United States. The Asian country of Bangladesh, for example, has 253 teen-age childbirths per 1,000. In sub-Sahara Africa, almost all the countries have rates of more than 100 per 1,000. In Eastern Europe, the countries of Bulgaria, Hungary, and Romania have higher teen-childbirth rates as well.

The Effect
of Statistics
Numbers can tell you much about an issue. You've just read a lot of numbers about teen pregnancy, data indicating that America is experiencing an explosion of children having children. But there are also problems with numbers. They make it easy to forget that real lives are involved here—the lives of teenagers. These are kids just like you. Their futures are being changed, and the futures of their children remain uncertain. Everyone involved in dealing with a teen pregnancy is greatly affected physically, emotionally, and financially. The teens get the brunt of the pain and must deal with most of the problems, but few parents and other close family members are left untouched. In many cases, family members must bear an extra financial burden, in addition to having to take on new responsibilities required by a baby. So with all these problems, why are so many teenagers becoming pregnant?

3

. . . . . .

Why Is Teen Pregnancy on the Rise?

Why weren't they careful? Why didn't they wait? Some believed they were in love. Some thought, "Everyone else is doing it." Others didn't realize it could happen to them. Some didn't think about it at all. "It didn't enter my mind about getting pregnant," said one teen mother. There are several reasons for these attitudes: peer pressure, sexual ignorance, the media, poverty, and broken homes.

Sex Sells

Many people believe that the media— especially television—is partly to blame. A large percentage of teenagers spend more time in front of the television than they do in the classroom. The average American family has

Madonna performs live in concert, wearing a sexually suggestive outfit. Many people argue that the great emphasis on sex in American culture has encouraged teens to become sexually active earlier.

the television turned on 7 hours a day. Teenagers watch about 24 hours of television a week. Their behavior shows what they have learned from this video "teacher." Television programs and advertisements bombard viewers with sex. One study showed that in a single year there were 20,000 sexual messages on television. Sex is used to sell almost anything you can imagine—cars, travel, soft drinks, toothpaste, clothing. Television shows six times more extramarital sex (sex outside marriage) than sex between husbands and wives. More than 90 percent of the sexual encounters on soap operas are between people not married to each other.

Many teenagers believe that television presents an accurate picture of pregnancy and the results of sex. A large number of teens say that they do not use birth control because they are "swept away" by

Do Teens Want to Have Babies?

In 1984, journalist Leon Dash decided to write about teenage pregnancy for the *Washington Post*. As many people believed, and still believe, he thought teenagers became pregnant because they did not understand reproduction. His study showed otherwise.

For his book *When Children Want Children: The Urban Crisis of Teenage Childbearing*, Dash interviewed a number of teenage girls. They started out telling one story—that they did not understand birth control or that they were tricked by older boys. When Dash won their trust, however, many of the girls admitted the truth. They wanted to have babies. They understood exactly what they were doing. Most of them were doing poorly in school. They knew they would probably not graduate. They decided there was no reason to postpone motherhood. "These girls have babies because they want someone to love them back, no questions asked," concluded Dash.

passion. This surely reflects the romanticized view of sex that television gives.

Peer Pressure

"If you love me, you'll do it."

"Everyone's doing it."

"It's no big deal. What are you afraid of?"

"Sex isn't about love anymore," says one teenage boy. "There's such peer pressure to do it." The star tackle of the football team can usually get any girl that he wants, but one star tackle isn't looking for action. For the past year, Richard has been dating Dyana. They went out for eight months before they went to bed together. Waiting this long was very unusual in their group, but they wanted to make sure sex would be right emotionally. The pregnancy rate among teens is so high in their community that a birth-control clinic has been set up opposite the high school. "A lot of guys say they won't spend more than two weeks with a girl—if she won't sleep with them, they drop her," Richard comments. "My friends couldn't understand why we waited so long. They gave me a really hard time about it."

Many teens are pushed by their friends into doing something they are not ready for and really don't understand. Peer pressure can be a very strong and persuasive force for sexual relations during adolescence. This is especially true when it is combined with the power of the media. But there are also a number of other reasons why so many teenagers become parents.

Someone to Love Me

"My parents don't care about me, and the kids at school don't like me. A baby will love me, no matter what."

"No one thinks I can do anything right—but I can. I can have a baby. That shows someone loves me."

"People will start to respect me once I have a baby of my own."

Jennifer wanted a child. "I'd been fighting with my mother for as long as I can remember. We never got along. I wanted someone to love and to love me back. I never got the love I wanted from my mother. She always seemed too busy for me. I used to try to get her attention. I wanted to yell, 'I need you! Look at me!' I started fooling around just to be close to someone. I didn't like the sex part. I liked being cuddled."

Sexual Ignorance

"My stomach hurts," 16-year-old Kelley, a junior at a New York high school, told the nurse. It wasn't hard for the nurse to find the problem. Kelley was eight months pregnant. She had no idea that she was expecting a child.

Opposite:
Many teens say that they became pregnant because they were careless in a moment of passion. Studies, however, show that many teens want to have babies so that they can have someone to take care of and love.

Some teen pregnancies can be attributed to ignorance about birth-control devices and their proper use. Below are (from top to bottom) a month's supply of birth-control pills, a condom, and a diaphragm.

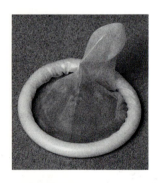

Not every teenager who gets pregnant is like Kelley. "Most teenagers don't want to get pregnant," according to Maris Vinovskis, who was one of President Bush's advisers on teen pregnancy. "They do not understand birth control."

Faye Wattleton agrees. She is the past president of Planned Parenthood. "America's youth are sexually illiterate," she says. The numbers that she cites are convincing. How many teenagers use birth-control devices? Only 33 percent! That means 67 percent of sexually active teens are *not* using birth control. And if they are using it, it may not be correctly. Robert Johnson, a New Jersey doctor, agrees as well. He tells the story of a teenage couple who got birth-control pills and knew nothing about how to use them. Instead of just the girl taking them, the boy took them one month, and the girl took them the next month. That way, they explained, they could share the responsibility.

Marie McFadden is a nurse at the Teen Health Center at Cambridge Ridge and Latin School in Cambridge, Massachusetts. The school began giving out condoms in the early 1990s. "Most of the kids have a lot of questions, because they don't know very much," she said. "And almost everyone who asks for condoms is already sexually active. I've talked to only a handful of kids who were thinking about having sex for the first time."

Joanne Rocco Bruno is the director of Planned Parenthood in eastern Pennsylvania. After surveying 2,500 teenagers, she found that 45 percent were unable to answer questions about reproduction and birth control. Here are some of the most common mistaken ideas:

- No one gets pregnant having sex the first time.
- You can get pregnant by kissing.
- Some days are 100 percent safe; you can never get pregnant then.
- You can't get pregnant if you dance or jump up and down right after having sex.

How can we wipe out this ignorance? There aren't that many places where kids can get facts about sex or birth-control devices. Many are not willing to speak to their parents. Their parents may not be comfortable talking about sex either. Their friends don't know the facts, so kids turn to school. In 1974, only 5 states and the District of Columbia required sex-education programs in public schools. By 1989, 16 states and the District of Columbia required them, and 24 other states encouraged school districts to offer them.

Since the early 1980s, about 150 junior and senior high schools have set up school-based clinics that dispense birth-control information and devices or refer teens to outside sources. Clearly, that leaves a lot of kids with no way to get the facts.

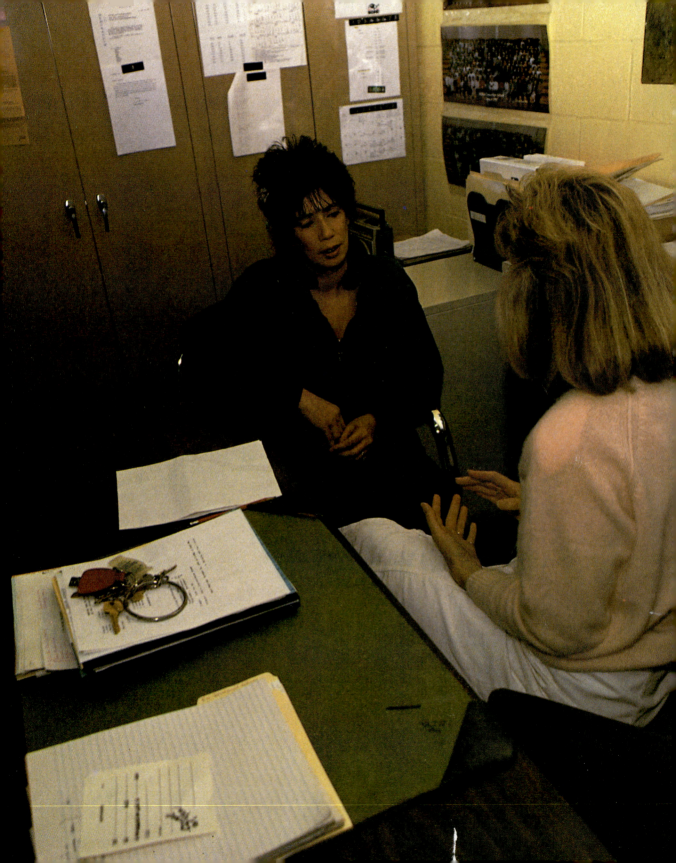

Norplant: A New Birth-Control Device

A new kind of birth-control device, different from all other devices on the market, was recently developed. Called Norplant, it is surgically implanted in the skin under the arm of a female. It lasts five years.

In December of 1992, a spokesperson for Laurence Paquin High School in Baltimore, Maryland, said that it would offer Norplant to girls who wanted it. Why Baltimore? Because it has one of the nation's highest teen-pregnancy rates. "We look at Norplant as just another service we offer these girls," says Rosetta Stith, Laurence Paquin's principal. If the program is successful, Baltimore hopes to include Norplant in all eight of its clinics in both high schools and middle schools.

Many teens feel that they are getting a mixed message about birth control. "Most of them feel it's a bad idea to have a child at their age," said one counselor, "but they have picked up on adults' mixed feelings about birth control. In other countries, birth-control devices are openly advertised on television. The message is clear. Teens in this country get mixed messages. They are warned to be careful, but their access to birth control is limited."

Norplant implants are surgically placed under the skin of a female.

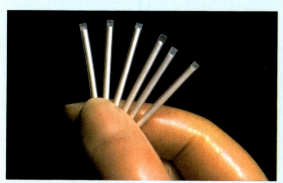

Low-Income Families

A number of studies have shown that teen pregnancy, while not limited to the poor, is more widespread among teens who live in poverty. Poor teenage girls have fewer choices than those from upper-income families. They also see less reason for remaining in school and putting off parenthood. They are less likely to find jobs.

These girls tend to feel hopeless. They feel that they have no control over the course of their own lives. In the April 1989 issue of *Harper's* magazine, reporter Elizabeth Marek told of visiting a group of

Opposite:
One of the best ways to overcome ignorance about sexual matters is to seek advice from others. Parents and counselors can often provide the most reliable and accurate information.

teenage mothers in the Bronx, New York. "I hear again and again how little control these girls feel they have over the events of their lives." "I have about as much control over my life as a leaf falling from a tree," said one girl.

"The biggest roadblock to breaking the cycle of poverty is this mentality of no hope," said the director of a program for teenage mothers. It is very hard to convince someone who has no hope that it's important to prepare for the future, to put off having children. It's hard to see the value of going to work and setting aside money before raising a family.

Broken
Homes
Families are under enormous strain. In many instances, children grow up on their own, without adequate guidance. More than 40 percent of today's teenagers live in single-parent homes. Between one quarter and one third of these kids are "latchkey children." They go home to empty houses because their parents are at work. Fourteen percent have unmarried parents. Many teen mothers themselves come from broken homes. Too few believe in themselves—or in the ability of adults to make wise choices.

They have frequently been let down in the past. "Many of these girls feel alienated from life," says Marcia Spector, executive director of the Suffolk

Raising a child can put great strains on young marriages. A number of teen marriages break up as a result of the pressures of child care and the added financial burden.

Network on Adolescent Pregnancy in Long Island, New York. "Having a baby gives them an anchor, gives them purpose, responsibility, and control." One young mother agrees. "Having a baby makes you grow up faster," says Jackie, 17, the mother of 18-month-old Nicole. Softly, she adds, "I feel older than I am."

How does having a baby affect a parent's life? Let's take a look at some of the problems that teen mothers and fathers experience.

4

The Problems

There's nothing new about young girls having babies. Historically, marriage and childbearing come early in many cultures. What *is* new is our awareness of the problems that early childbearing brings. Having children when you're a teenager affects your health and the child's, too. It also causes economic and social problems.

"Teen pregnancy is a roadblock to all kinds of things for young people, and the younger it happens, the more of a roadblock it is," says Ron O'Brien of the Children's Defense Group. The teenagers who become pregnant are often those who can least afford a child. Frequently they are poor and cannot get good medical care.

Hal Warden, 15, was a father for the first time when he was only 13. Here, he poses for a family portrait with his second wife, Catherine, and his two children.

Typically they live in a one-parent family. They don't do well in school—and probably will not graduate. They cannot get good jobs, and they feel frustrated and hopeless. Like dominoes tumbling over one another, everything in a young girl's life can suddenly come crashing down around her when she has a baby.

Health

Risks Pregnancy poses greater health risks to teenagers than to women in their twenties. Teen mothers are more likely to die during childbirth. There's a 13 percent greater chance that a youngster between the ages of 15 and 19 will die while giving birth than a woman in her twenties. The death rate is highest for teens under the age of 14. They are 60 percent more likely to die in childbirth than if they became pregnant in their twenties. Their children are also in greater danger.

The younger you are, the greater the risk for your baby. Babies born to teens or preteens are two to three times more likely to die in their first year than babies born to women in their twenties. Younger mothers have a higher rate of giving birth prematurely. There is also a greater chance of stillbirths (births of dead babies) and of low-weight babies. About 17 percent of the children born to teenagers are of low birth weight. This is because teenage

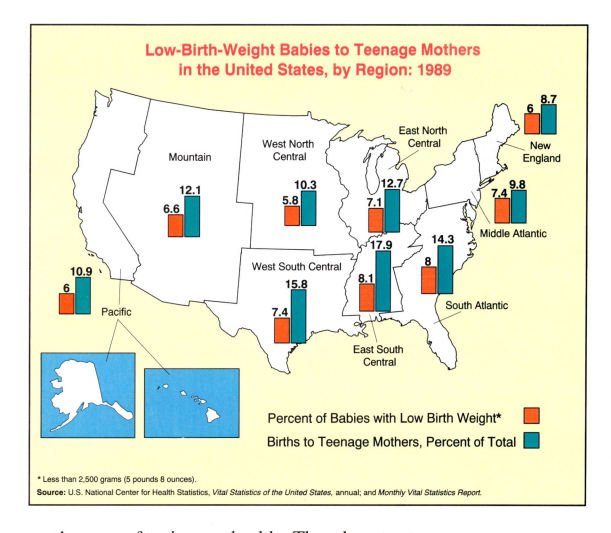

Low-Birth-Weight Babies to Teenage Mothers in the United States, by Region: 1989

New England: 6, 8.7

Mountain: 6.6, 12.1

West North Central: 5.8, 10.3

East North Central: 7.1, 12.7

Middle Atlantic: 7.4, 9.8

Pacific: 6, 10.9

West South Central: 7.4, 15.8

East South Central: 8.1, 17.9

South Atlantic: 8, 14.3

Percent of Babies with Low Birth Weight*

Births to Teenage Mothers, Percent of Total

* Less than 2,500 grams (5 pounds 8 ounces).

Source: U.S. National Center for Health Statistics, *Vital Statistics of the United States,* annual; and *Monthly Vital Statistics Report.*

mothers are often in poor health. They do not eat properly or get adequate medical care. Low birth weight is a major cause of illness among newborns. In addition, it contributes to children having such birth defects as mental retardation, blindness, and deafness.

These problems can place the infants at serious developmental risk—they may not grow as well.

Marian Wright Edelman and the CDF

Marian Wright Edelman

her organization—has grown enormously. Today, in addition to lobbying lawmakers, the CDF undertakes certain campaigns of its own. The CDF believes that preventing pregnancy at a young age will help break a cycle of poverty and lack of education that has created many of America's problems. Another function of the CDF is to do research and compile statistics on the nation's teen-pregnancy problem. Below and opposite are two ads that the CDF uses to show young people how serious the problem of teen pregnancy in America really is.

In 1973, a lawyer named Marian Wright Edelman founded the Children's Defense Fund (CDF) in Washington, D.C. Her goal was to create an institution that would be a strong voice in the government for America's 60 million children—many of whom are poor and uneducated. The CDF began to lobby lawmakers in an effort to convince them to fund programs that would help feed and educate the nation's neediest youth.

Since the CDF's founding, Marian Wright Edelman's influence—and the influence of

AN EXTRA SEVEN POUNDS COULD KEEP YOU OFF THE FOOTBALL TEAM.

Become a father before you're ready and you may always wonder what else you could have been.
THE CHILDREN'S DEFENSE FUND

It's like being grounded for eighteen years.

Having a baby when you're a teenager takes away more than your freedom, it takes away your dreams.

The Children's Defense Fund.

Some Facts from the Children's Defense Fund

- Every 31 seconds an infant is born to an unmarried mother.

- Every 55 seconds an infant is born to a mother who is not a high school graduate.

- Every 32 seconds a teen between the ages of 15 and 19 becomes pregnant.

- Every 64 seconds an infant is born to a teenager.

Opposite:
Studies have shown that girls who become pregnant while in school are much less likely to get a diploma than those who don't get pregnant. This lack of education later translates into fewer job opportunities and lower incomes.

Babies with low birth weights can have trouble learning. They may not be able to concentrate. Dr. Janet Hardy is a professor of pediatrics in Baltimore, Maryland, who studied the children of girls 16 or younger. She wanted to see how well these children did in school. She gave them an IQ test, a method of testing intelligence. A score of 100 is average. A child with a score of 70 or below is considered retarded. Here's what she found when she tested the kindergarten children of teen mothers:

- 11 percent scored 70 or below, compared with 2.6 percent of the general population.
- Only 5 percent scored above 110, compared with 25 percent of all U.S. children.

What does this mean? The children of teenage mothers are starting out with some big strikes against them. Another domino falls.

Dropping Out

of School How many teenage mothers finish high school? Here are some disturbing facts.

The graph on page 44 shows that the younger a girl is when she becomes a mother, the less likely she is to complete high school by the time she reaches her twenties. Teen males who become fathers before they are 18 are 40 percent less likely to graduate from high school than those who wait.

Children born into poverty or a very stressful family often have a wide variety of physical and emotional problems. These problems can delay normal social and intellectual development, which, in turn, can hurt their abilities to succeed in school. Most educators believe that children who are likely to drop out can be clearly identified by the third grade! For children who start out with these disadvantages, school becomes a long downward spiral.

Few Job

Opportunities The more education you have, the more likely you are to get a good job. This is especially true when times are tough. In 1975, about 8 million teens were employed. During the early 1990s, only 6 million had jobs. In 1980, there were 1 million jobs for teenagers that were paid for by the federal government. By the 1990s, there were fewer than 750,000 federal jobs. The figures

Opposite:
Competition for jobs in America is tough. A high school diploma and some solid work experience are usually required for most jobs with decent pay.

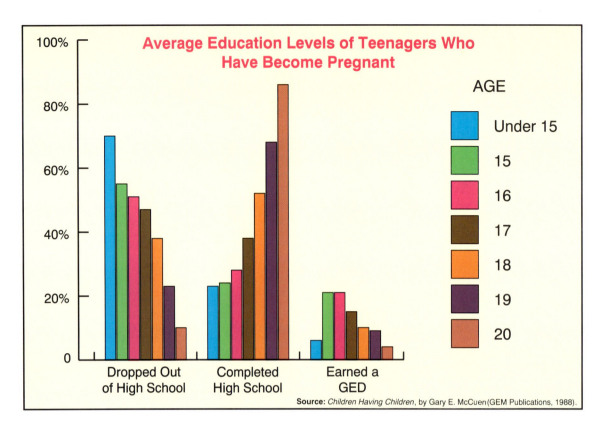

Average Education Levels of Teenagers Who Have Become Pregnant

AGE
- Under 15
- 15
- 16
- 17
- 18
- 19
- 20

Dropped Out of High School | Completed High School | Earned a GED

Source: *Children Having Children*, by Gary E. McCuen (GEM Publications, 1988).

are even worse for America's minorities. More than 41 percent of African-American youths and 27 percent of Latino teens are without jobs. You read that teenage parents are less likely to finish school. They are also less likely to get a job. This can sink them even deeper into poverty and despair. The dominoes topple.

Poverty and Hopelessness

There is often a sad connection between poverty and teenage pregnancy. A large number of teen mothers grew up in poor homes. In many cases, they are themselves the children of teenage mothers. These young mothers may then raise their children in a similar environment. They continue the cycle of poverty. Says one director of a program for teen mothers, "The really serious problem is that most of these kids are not even developing the tools they need to take advantage of the opportunities available to them. They just don't have the drive or the role models or the motivation to break the cycle." A study conducted by the Attica Correctional Facility in Buffalo, New York, found that 90 percent of the prisoners had been born to teenage mothers.

Researcher Scott Fosler studied how the poor children of teenage mothers compare with the poor kids of the 1930s. He discovered that many of the children who grew up during the depression of the 1930s worked hard and became very successful. Today, many of the poor kids of teen parents have yet to make good. According to Fosler, it isn't a question of whether a family is poor that makes the difference, but "whether the kids are getting the kind of parenting and the motivation to overcome obstacles. Today, so many kids who are poor are not getting that kind of parenting. In many cases there is only one parent, a teen mother with a limited education. She is struggling to make ends meet. It's very difficult for kids in that situation to break out."

Experts see this as a big problem. "We can no longer let our kids stumble into parenting," states a recent report from the Center for Population Options. "Parenting is a course that should be embarked on only when one is ready, willing, and able to become a parent." But there's a lot more to the situation than that.

Unstable Marriages

As has already been noted, young girls who have babies undergo great financial and emotional hardships because of their early childbearing. Only one third ever get married. Very few marry the father of their first child. Seven out of 10 children born to mothers under age 18 live in single-parent homes. Divorce and separation are three times more likely to occur among teenagers than among older couples or couples who postpone childbearing until their twenties or later.

A Burden for Society

These results are harmful to individual teenagers, but the costs to society are staggering. Pregnant or teen mothers make up a huge portion of the welfare population. How much?

- More than $21.5 billion is spent every year on welfare, food stamps, and medical assistance for teen mothers and their babies.

- Each first birth to a teenager costs federal, state, and local governments an average of $18,700 every year for 20 years.
- By the time the babies born to teenagers reach the age of 20, it is estimated that the government will have spent more than $6 billion to support all of them together.
- A third of this money—more than $2 billion—could have been saved if teenage mothers had waited until they reached age 20 to have their first baby.

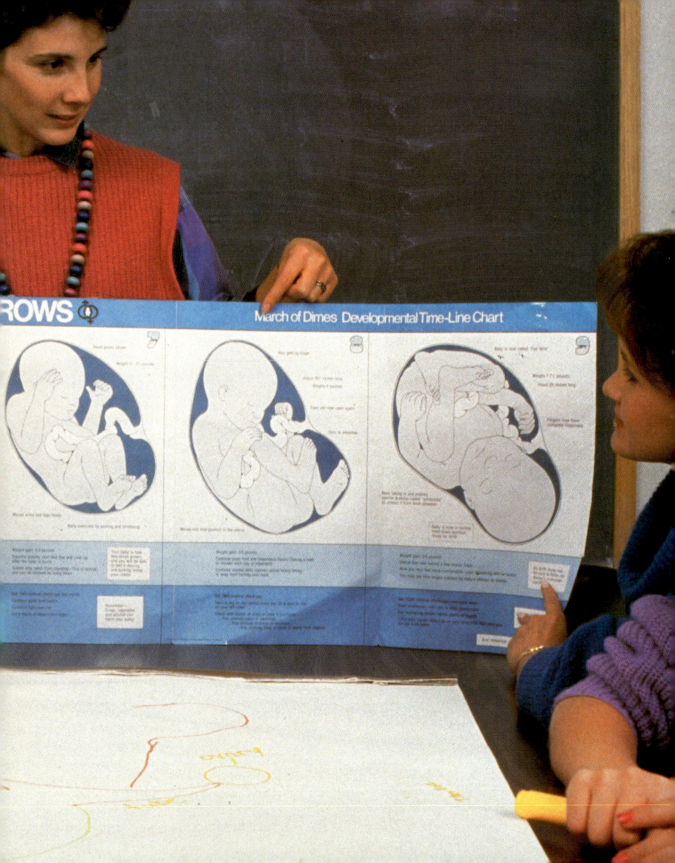

5

What Can Be Done?

You've read about teen pregnancies and the problems that pregnant teenagers face. Now, what can be done to halt the epidemic? Various sex-education programs, school-based clinics, and new types of schools are being tried. Some people think that moral values are the answer. Others have some very different ideas.

Sex Education

Does sex education reduce the number of teen pregnancies? Laurie Zabin is a professor at the Johns Hopkins University School of Public Health. She spent three years studying this problem. She looked at four Baltimore, Maryland, high schools, two that

Researchers have found that providing sex education to both teens and pre-teens significantly reduces the rates of teen pregnancy.

had sex education and two that did not. At the schools that did not have a program, the pregnancy rates rose 57.6 percent over the three-year period. What about the schools that did have a program? Pregnancy rates dropped 30.1 percent. "Schools are a place where you can change teenagers' behavior, and we know from existing studies that the answer [to the question, Does sex education make a difference?] can be yes," she concluded.

Researcher Joy Dryfoos agrees with Zabin. She reported a sharp decrease in the number of girls having babies at high schools with sex-education programs. Another researcher found that by the end of the eighth grade, girls who had not taken a sex-education course were five times more likely to have begun engaging in sexual relations than girls who had completed a course.

While most of the sex-education courses are aimed at girls, there are a number of programs for boys as well. For example, there is a program for teenage boys at the St. Luke's Medical Center in Chicago, Illinois. In 1983, the Bank Street College of Education in New York City established a Teen Father Project. Eight locations were selected where young men were given instruction in everything from how to change a diaper to how to get a job. As a result, these men gained a better understanding of the responsibilities of fatherhood.

School-Based

Clinics
Few issues are as touchy as schools giving out birth-control devices. How does the federal government react?

In 1987, Bill Clinton, who was then the governor of Arkansas, appointed Dr. Joycelyn Elders director of the Arkansas Department of Public Health. At a news conference, reporters asked Dr. Elders if she planned to give out birth-control devices in schools. "Well," she answered, "we're not going to put them on their lunch trays, but, yes." Five years later, when, as president-elect, Clinton nominated Dr. Elders for surgeon general of the United States, the question came up again. Dr. Elders stood by her earlier answer. "We would like to expand the school-based birth-control program," she said. "We have schools on the waiting list."

Dr. Elders has long crusaded against teenage pregnancy. She thinks that a poor teenager with a baby is "captive into a slavery the Thirteenth Amendment did not anticipate." There are many people who disagree with Dr. Elders, especially religious leaders, and they have vigorously attacked her policy. Dr. Elders fights back. "We are talking about life," she says. "What I saw in the many places my nurses took me, I don't define as living. We have nineteen-year-olds who already have five children. That's not life."

School boards around the country are debating the wisdom of handing out birth-control devices in their schools. For several years, about two dozen schools have been distributing birth-control devices through school-based clinics. However, the issue of schools giving out condoms did not get wide attention until the fall of 1992. That's when Joseph A. Fernandez, chancellor of New York City's public schools, announced that he wanted to make condoms available to all students in the city's 120 high schools. His progressive ideas on sex education provoked so much opposition that Fernandez resigned in 1993. Nonetheless, Fernandez's approach sparked a spirited debate about whether such action discourages or encourages sexual activity. The debate is still going on.

A number of school districts have rejected plans to distribute birth-control devices to teens. Mill Valley, California, and Talbolt County, Maryland, for example, decided such programs did not belong in school. "There's a real debate about what the role of the school should be," said Brenda Greene, manager of AIDS education at the National School Boards Association. Many school officials, parents, teachers, and students believe that kids need protection against pregnancy. They argue that since teens don't need parental consent to buy condoms, school programs shouldn't require it either. On the other

Opposite:
Dr. Joycelyn Elders, President Clinton's nominee for U.S. surgeon general, is a strong supporter of school-based birth-control clinics.

hand, religious leaders and a number of parents and teachers argue that handing out birth-control devices encourages premarital sex. Because of this, most school districts require teens to obtain their parents' permission to get condoms.

Special Schools

How can teen mothers and their children break out of the cycle of poverty and hopelessness? Many people feel that education is the answer. More and more cities are offering programs that enable pregnant teens or teenage mothers to stay in school. The mothers can leave their children in day care while they go to classes. The day care is right there in the building, which makes it much easier. Let's look at one of these programs.

The Educational Program for Pregnant and Parenting Adolescents (EPPPA) in Oakdale, New York, is a public high school. The EPPPA provides the young girls enrolled in it with parenting classes, child care, counseling, prenatal health services, plus eight periods each week of academics. For some of the girls, this kind of school environment is nothing short of salvation. The daily grind can be rough, however. Teachers and other members of the staff emphasize graduating from high school, getting ready to take a job, and going to college. They tell the girls to be proud, focus on achieving, and to

Opposite:
While he served as the chancellor of New York City's public schools, Joseph A. Fernandez tried to create a program of condom distribution in high schools.

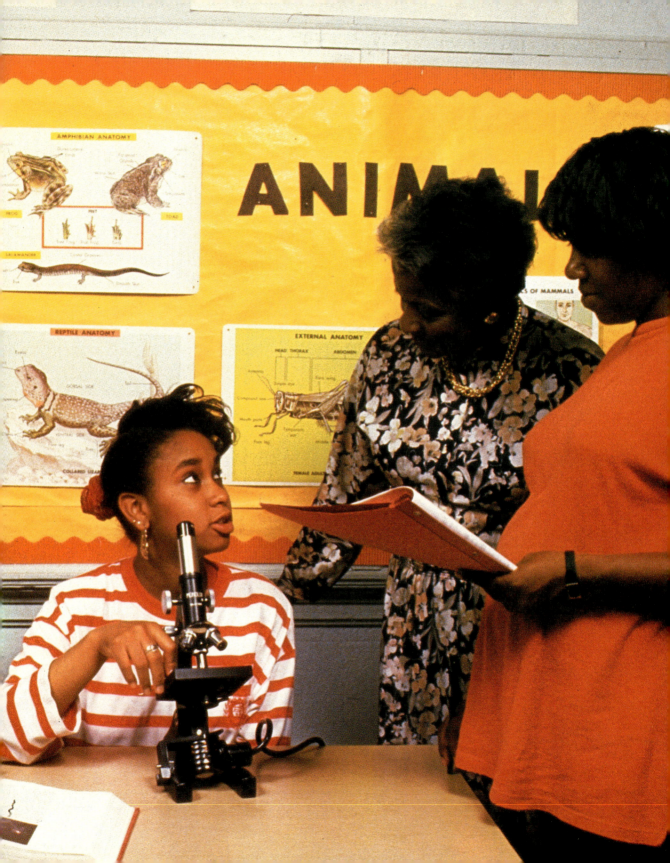

work hard. Reassurance is what keeps many of these young people going.

Just Say No!

What about old-fashioned morality? Sandra Hofferth, a researcher at the Urban Institute in Washington, D.C., studied the relationship between attending weekly religious services and putting off sexual activity. She found that girls who went to church often were much less likely to get pregnant. A number of other studies support her findings. Some people say that this is too simple an answer for a complicated problem. Others say that it's time to preach values once again.

The Buck Stops Here

Some states have taken unusual approaches to the teen-pregnancy problem. At Children's Hospital in Denver, Colorado, the chief of psychology tries to persuade teenage mothers to postpone having more children by paying them. The girls get a dollar a day for two years—one every day that they do not get pregnant. Each week, the girls get together to discuss their problems and anxieties. "These kids ought to know better," say people who are opposed to the program. "You're right," says the program's creator, Dr. Jeffrey Dolgan. "I look forward to the day when they do."

Opposite:
Students study biology at a special school for pregnant teens in North Carolina. Such schools offer young women a better chance to finish their educations and to prepare for their futures.

Critics can't argue with his success rate. Of the original group of 18 girls, only 3 got pregnant again within the two years. This is a rate of less than 17 percent. The nationwide rate is much higher: more than 40 percent of unmarried pregnant teenagers will get pregnant again within two years. Dolgan says, "The girls learn it's important to take time to grow up, so they'll have more to offer another child. That's a big realization for a sixteen-year-old. . . ."

In 1986, Wisconson passed a law requiring the parents of boys and girls under 18 to support their grandchildren if their children couldn't. Lawmakers hope this will encourage families to take greater responsibility for their children's upbringing.

Combined

Efforts
Clearly there are many approaches to tackling the issue of teen pregnancy. Whatever the approaches are, however, it is certain that they must address a number of complex and long-standing problems. Educators must make sure that teens understand the consequences of having sex. Parents, community leaders, and counselors must keep the lines of communication open with teens. And, most important, society must not allow its youth to take lightly the awesome responsibility of having babies or to ignore the fact that becoming a parent is a decision that affects a person for a lifetime.

Opposite:
Many states and cities offer special teen hot lines that can help young people better cope with the stresses of life. For pregnant teens and teen parents, these services can often provide much needed comfort and a new perspective for the future.

Glossary

abortion A method of ending a pregnancy.

adolescent A teenager; a person who is between the ages of 12 and 18.

adoption The legal raising of a child by either one or two people who are not the birth parents.

broken home A family that is split up as a result of divorce, separation, or the desertion of one parent.

condom A birth-control device.

epidemic The rapid spread of a disease or problem to a large number of people.

extramarital sex Sexual relations with someone other than one's husband or wife.

GED Stands for "general equivalency diploma," which is recognized as a high school diploma.

implant To surgically insert something into the body.

IQ Stands for "intelligence quotient." An IQ test measures intelligence.

media Television, radio, newspapers, magazines, and other forms of communication that reach many people.

Norplant A birth-control device that is surgically inserted into a female's arm.

peer pressure Force or strong demands by people of one's own age to behave in a certain way.

reproductive system The organs in the body that make the creation of offspring possible.

sex education A course that provides young people with the facts about sexual relations, pregnancy, and birth-control devices and gives them information about the problems related to these issues.

stillbirth The birth of a dead baby.

Thirteenth Amendment The amendment to the U.S. Constitution that prohibits slavery.

For Further Reading

Bode, Jane. *Kids Still Having Kids: Talk About Teen Pregnancy.* New York: Franklin Watts, 1980.

Gase, Linda. "Pregnant Teens." *Teen Magazine,* December 1991, p. 22.

Hammerslough, Jane. *Teen Motherhood.* New York: The Rosen Publishing Group, 1992.

Hughes, Tracy. *Teen Pregnancy.* New York: The Rosen Publishing Group, 1992.

Jakobson, Cathryn. "In Trouble." *Seventeen,* April 1992, p. 142.

McCuen, Gary E. *Children Having Children.* Hudson, Wisconsin: GEM Publications, 1988.

Source Notes

Brody, Jane E. "Helping Teenagers Avoid Pregnancy." *The New York Times,* October 2, 1991, p. A14.

Bruning, Fred. "The Children on the Bus." *Newsday.* April 20, 1992, pp. 42–43.

Cantwell, Mary. "After an 18-Year Decline, Teenage Births Are Up." *The New York Times,* January 29, 1989, p. 81.

Dash, Leon. *When Children Want Children: The Urban Crisis of Teenage Childbearing.* New York: William Morrow and Company, 1989.

Marek, Elizabeth. "The Lives of Teenage Mothers: School-books, Boyfriends, and Babies." *Harper's,* April 1989, p. 55.

McAnarey, Elizabeth R., and Hendee, William R. "The Prevention of Adolescent Pregnancy." *The Journal of the American Medical Association,* July 7, 1989, p. 78.

McCuen, Gary E. *Children Having Children.* Hudson, WI: GEM Publications, 1988.

Perry, Nancy L. "Why It's So Tough to Be a Girl." *Fortune,* August 19, 1992, p. 82.

Shapiro, Joseph P. "The Teen Pregnancy Boom." *U.S. News & World Report,* July 13, 1992, p. 39.

Index